1 Marcel and Céline are French mice. (Marcel is a detective and Céline is a painter.) One summer they go to Los Angeles on holiday.

2 They take a bus from the airport to Hollywood.

3 Céline looks at the map.

1

4 They walk to Maytree Avenue. Then...

5

Number 28 – this is it.

Do you want to know about the Waldmans? This says: 'Arnold is a film director, and Claudia comes from Italy.'

Their daughter Lois, is fifteen years old....

6 Marcel opens the door and goes in.

Look, Céline There's the door to our holiday flat.

The photos in *Hollywood Holidays* were right.

Yes, this is Beautiful.

7 At ten o'clock Marcel and Céline go to bed. But at twelve o'clock Marcel opens his eyes again. He can hear a noise.

8 He goes upstairs to the kitchen.

9 Then he sees a note.

10 In the morning, Arnold and Claudia Waldman read the note, too.

11 The Waldmans talk for a long time. Then at 9.15 Arnold leaves for his office. Marcel and Céline go, too.

12 Arnold drives to the Silver Star Film Studios.

13 At 9.45.

14 In his office, the film director walks up and down.

15 The telephone rings. Arnold answers it.

18 Arnold leaves his office at 10.15. Marcel and Céline go, too.
First he goes shopping and buys a suitcase. After that he goes to his bank and puts $1 million in the suitcase. Then he drives to Long Beach. At 11.55...

19 Arnold finds room 309 on the Queen Mary. A man with red hair opens the door to him.

Arnold Waldman?

Yes, that's me.

20 Suddenly ...

That's a big ship!

Ssshh!

It's all there. Now – where's my daughter? Is she OK?

Yes, she's OK... now. But this is only the first million. You don't get her back today.

22 Arnold leaves. Then the kidnapper telephones a friend.

23 At 2.15.

24 At 6.30 the car stops at an old house.
Marcel looks at Céline. Céline looks at Marcel.
It's very quiet. Then Stan takes the suitcase into the house.

25 He puts the suitcase on the table and opens it. 'Look at that!' says Chuck. The two men smile, but they don't look *under* the money. They go into the kitchen.

26 At eleven o'clock Stan and Chuck are sleeping. Then...

27 Marcel and Céline find Lois in a small bedroom. She's on the bed and she can't move.

28 Marcel and Céline go downstairs again. Then...

29 Very quietly, Marcel gives the guns to Céline.

30 Then, Marcel and Céline take the telephone upstairs.

31 In the bathroom, Marcel telephones the police.

34 Marcel and Céline walk to a bus-stop near the house. They wait there. They wait and wait. No buses come. 'It's very early in the morning,' says Marcel. Then he looks across the road and sees a big lorry.

Look! That lorry's going to Los Angeles.

He and Céline run to the lorry and get on it.

35 Later...

36 The lorry stops near Sunset Boulevard. From there, Marcel and Céline walk to 28 Maytree Avenue. They eat some fruit and drink a lot of coffee. Then...

Marcel! Is that Lois?

Yes. The police are bringing her home. A lot of TV and newspaper people are with them.

37 Lois talks to the TV and newspaper people. Marcel and Céline watch. But only for a short time. Then they swim in the Waldmans' pool.

Of course they are happy. It's hot... The sky is blue... And they *are* in Hollywood!

ACTIVITIES

Pages 1–7

Before you read

1 Read the Word List at the back of the book. What are the twenty words in your language?

2 Look at the pictures on pages 1 and 2. What do you think?
   a Is Marcel a man or a mouse?
   b What is Marcel and Céline's address in Hollywood?
   c A family lives in the house, too. What is their name?
   d Are Marcel and Céline there for work or for a holiday?

While you read

3 Are these sentences right (✓) or wrong (✗)?
   a Los Angeles is in Texas.   .....
   b Marcel and Céline take a bus to Hollywood.   .....
   c Arnold Waldman is a film director.   .....
   d On the first night, Marcel sees two kidnappers.   .....
   e The kidnappers leave a note.   .....
   f The kidnappers telephone Arnold in the morning.   .....
   g They want $1 million.   .....
   h They want the money at the studio.   .....

After you read

4 Work with a friend.
   a *Student A*: You want a flat in Hollywood for a holiday. Ask about the flat in Maytree Avenue.

      Student B: You work for Hollywood Holidays. Answer questions about the flat.
   b *Student A*: You are Arnold. You are reading the kidnappers' note. Talk to Claudia about it.

      Student B: You are Claudia. Ask about the note. What are you and Arnold going to do? Talk about it.

Pages 8–15

Before you read

5 Look at the pictures on page 8. Answer the questions.

    a What does Arnold Waldman take to the Queen Mary?

    b Who does he give it to?

    c What has the man in the blue shirt got in his hand?

While you read

6 Finish these sentences. Write one word.

    a Arnold .... his office at 10.15.

    b He buys a .... and puts $1 million in it.

    c The .... on the Queen Mary isn't happy with the money.

    d At 6.30 the kidnapper's car stops at an old ....

    e Marcel and Céline find .... upstairs.

    f They put Stan and Chuck's .... in the kitchen.

    g In the bathroom, Marcel telephones the ....

    h The police arrive at .... o'clock.

    i Lois goes home and the two mice can have their ....

After you read

7 A note, a ship, an old house and a lorry are all important in the story. Why?

8 You are Céline or Marcel. Write to a friend in Paris. Are you having a good holiday? Do you like Hollywood? Write about Lois and the kidnappers.

9 What do the newspapers say about Lois? Work with a friend and write the story.

Answers for the Activities in this book are available from the Pearson English Readers website. A free Activity Worksheet is also available from the website. Activity worksheets are part of the Pearson English Readers Teacher Support Programme, which also includes Progress tests and Graded Reader Guidelines. For more information, please visit: www.pearsonenglishreaders.com

WORD LIST *with example sentences*

avenue (n) She has a very expensive flat on Fifth *Avenue* in New York.

bathroom (n) The house has four bedrooms and two *bathrooms*.

detective (n) Hercule Poirot is a *detective* in some of Agatha Christie's stories.

downstairs (adv) Was that a noise in the kitchen? Can you go *downstairs* and see?

film director (n) Stephen Spielberg is a famous *film director*.

gun (n) Don't move! I've got a *gun*!

kidnapper (n) The little boy is at home again, but did they give money to his *kidnappers*?

leave (v) I'm *leaving* work now, but I'm going to be late.

lorry (n) The new table and chairs arrived in a big *lorry*.

map (n) This is a *map* of the town. Here, on the left, is the station.

mouse (n; pl **mice**) There are *mice* in the house. I can hear them at night.

million (number) I'd like one of those pictures in my house, but I haven't got £10 *million*!

note (n) There is *note* from your sister on the table. She is going to eat at a friend's house.

painter (n) He is a *painter*, but people don't buy his pictures.

pool (n) They are swimming in the *pool* in the garden.

ring (v) Jenny can't go to school. I am going to *ring* her teacher.

ship (n) We are on this *ship* because my mother doesn't like aeroplanes.

studio (n) They are making the film in a *studio* in London.

suitcase (n) You can only take one *suitcase* on the aeroplane.

upstairs (adv) She is going *upstairs* to bed.

Pearson Education Limited
Edinburgh Gate, Harlow,
Essex CM20 2JE, England
and Associated Companies throughout the world.

ISBN: 978-1-4058-7674-2

First published by Penguin Books 2000
This edition first published by Pearson Education 2008

15

Copyright © Stephen Rabley 2008
Illustrations by Inga Moore

Typeset by Graphicraft Ltd, Hong Kong
Set in 12/14pt Bembo
Printed in China
SWTC/15

Published by Pearson Education Ltd

*Every effort has been made to trace the copyright holders and we apologise in advance for any unintentional omissions.
We would be pleased to insert the appropriate acknowledgement in any subsequent edition of this publication.*

For a complete list of the titles available in the Pearson English Readers series, please visit
www.pearsonenglishreaders.com.
Alternatively, write to your local Pearson Education office or to Pearson English Readers
Marketing Department, Pearson Education, Edinburgh Gate, Harlow, Essex CM20 2JE, England.